When Jesus Was Born

Sharon Mullen • Illustrated by Bill Hutchinson

Broadman Press
Nashville, Tennessee

To
My husband, Carl
who loves to teach preschoolers

© Copyright 1987 • Broadman Press
All rights reserved.
4241-77

ISBN: 0-8054-4177-8
Library of Congress Catalog Card Number: 86-17552
Dewey Decimal Classification: C232.921
Subject Heading: JESUS CHRIST—NATIVITY

Printed in the United States of America

Library of Congress Cataloging-in-Publication Data

Mullen, Sharon, 1941-
　When Jesus was born.

　　(Bible-and-me)
　Summary: Presents the events surrounding Jesus's birth and early childhood.
　　1. Jesus Christ—Nativity—Juvenile literature.
[1. Jesus Christ—Nativity]　I. Title.　II. Hutchinson, William M., ill.　III. Series.
BT315.2.M84　　1987　　　232.9′2　　　86-17552
ISBN 0-8054-4177-8

"Mary, I have some news," Joseph said.
"We must go to Bethlehem."

"Bethlehem, Bethlehem. We must go to Bethlehem," said Mary. She packed food and clothes for the trip.

"We must go to Bethlehem," said Joseph. He put the bags of food and clothes on the donkey's back.

Joseph helped Mary onto the donkey. They were ready to go to Bethlehem.

Joseph led the donkey. Clip, clop, clip, clop. The donkey walked on the road to Bethlehem.

Mary rode the donkey. Joseph led the donkey. "Soon we will be in Bethlehem," he told Mary.

There were many people in Bethlehem. The town was crowded. "I must find a place for us to stay," said Joseph.

Knock, knock. Joseph knocked on the door. "Do you have room for us?" he asked. "My wife is tired."

"I have no room. You may stay in my stable," the man said.

Mary and Joseph went to the stable. They saw the animals. They saw the clean hay. "We will stay here," they said.

Joseph found the manger where hay was kept for the animals. He put clean hay in the manger.

Baby Jesus was born. Mary held Baby Jesus. Joseph smiled at Mary and Baby Jesus.

"Thank You, God, for Baby Jesus," Mary and Joseph said.

Mary was happy. She held Baby Jesus. She wrapped Baby Jesus in warm cloths.

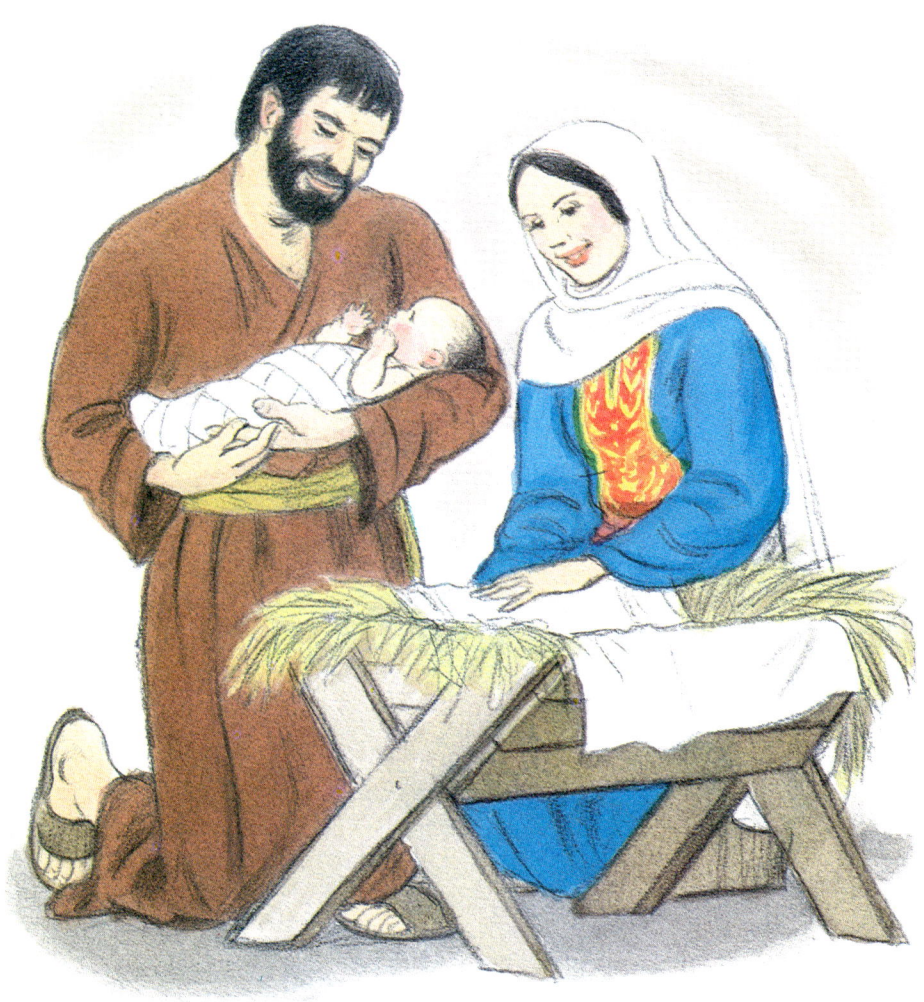

Joseph was happy. He held Baby Jesus. He laid Baby Jesus on the hay in the manger bed.

Shepherds were taking care of their sheep. They heard the good news. Baby Jesus was born in Bethlehem.

They went to Bethlehem to see Baby Jesus.

The shepherds found Mary and Joseph and Baby Jesus in the stable.

"Thank You, God, for bringing us to see Baby Jesus," the shepherds said.

Mary and Joseph took Baby Jesus to church.

People at church were happy to see Baby Jesus.

The Wise Men lived far from Bethlehem. They followed a star to Bethlehem. They were looking for Jesus.

The Wise Men stopped at a house in Bethlehem. This was where Joseph and Mary and Jesus lived.

The Wise Men brought presents for Jesus.

"Thank You, God, for bringing us to Jesus," they said.

"Jesus is growing," Mary said. Jesus helped Mary make bread.

"Jesus is growing," Joseph said. Jesus helped Joseph feed the animals.

Mary and Joseph taught Jesus about God.
"God loves us," Mary and Joseph said.
"God loves us," Jesus said.